Invisible City

volumes in the collection of current poetry
edited by John McBride & Paul Vangelisti

0 : *the first 25*

1 : *Humps & Wings: Polish poetry since '68*

2 : *Italian Poetry, 1960–1980 :*
from Neo to Post Avant-garde

3 : *Abandoned Latitudes: new writing*
by 3 Los Angeles poets

  etc (details at rear)

Abandoned Latitudes

new writing by 3 Los Angeles poets –
John Thomas, Robert Crosson & Paul Vangelisti
with an introduction by Giulia Niccolai
and photographs by Jeffrey Scales

Invisible City | 3
San Francisco & Los Angeles

Some of these works first appeared in *Invisible City,*
Zeta (Udine) and *Boxcar.*

Grants from the California Arts Council and the
National Endowment for the Arts (a federal agency)
aided the publication of this volume.

Designed by John McBride
& printed in the USA

Library of Congress card catalog number 83-060078
ISBN 0-88031-062-6

The Red Hill Press
PO Box 2853
San Francisco, California 94126

3 abandoned latitudes seen from abroad

In most languages, I should think, the name 'Patagonia' sounds like a joke. Redundant and ridiculous. In Italian the expression: 'Ma va in Patagonia...' used to mean 'Go chase yourself.' I remember hearing it as a child, I remember myself being told to go to Patagonia, but I have the feeling the expression has since gone out of use. Why? Because in the jet age Patagonia can actually be reached (whereas before, at least in Italy, it had a connotation of absolute unreachability), or because, more subjectively, not being a child anymore no one wishes me there any longer?

Still, the first impulse on reading Thomas' 'Patagonia' is to yell out to him: 'Hi John, I'm in Patagonia too!'

We all would like to be in Thomas' Patagonia because Patagonia is fun and it is a highly professional, charted state-of-well-being in time and space. It is the right place to be. Patagonia is *in*. And we can't help but cry over spilt milk: 'Why have we been so haphazard instead, so unbelieving and hit-or-miss in building our own Patagonian Empire?' Why have *I* wasted so much time with castles in the air while Thomas was working at Patagonia like Saint Theresa or a construction company? There he is, at the back of his shack with the penguins aligned. The background is grey, barren, hilly and windy. The two girls I catch a glimpse of through the open kitchen window. How right that there should be two of them (Raquel and Lili) and not one or three or whatever. It's not a harem and it's not love and there's a wide age gap between the girls and the 'I' who is writing. Humbert and Lolita thirty years later *do* come to mind.... But, did I just write: '... it's not love'? Who am *I* to say that? I take it right back.

Learning to be scrupulous in these matters – thanks to Thomas – I am now asking myself whether I know where Patagonia is. I don't. Shall I look it up in the *Encyclopaedia Britannica Atlas* with its beautifully pragmatic motto on the title page: 'The Whole World Is Here – Unabridged'?

From the names in the text, their quality of *Ora pro nobis* litany: 'Punta Arenas Río Verde San Gregorio Punta Delgada' I have been visualizing Patagonia somewhere between Spanish-speaking Latin America and the silent (?) South Pole.

Writing this down has brought another association to mind: the Falkland-Malvinas War.

The atlas shows me how close they are.

How close are we to reality when we venture to say that it is Thomas' writing of 'Patagonia' which caused the Argentina-England war?

Before it actually took place who could have ever ventured to believe that Argentina and England would have gone to war?

It would be very naïve to say that Patagonia is the metaphor of a 'private niche.'

It is more reasonable to say that life is the metaphor of Patagonia.

A Poem for Bob Crosson

So America acknowledges
So Italy does 2.
Cryptic me
Cryptic you.
A wet check.
Check: I wrote it right.
I wrote it wet.
Dream! (Imperative).
We all do
And smoke Lucky Strikes.

A Sort of Poem   A Poem of Sorts

Waiter   and   Waited on.
(Apropos of Wet Check).

Or a Sort of Introduction (Anonymous)

At last S.P. lives. In Cervantes merely an illiterate servant-accessory of the hero, he has now been brought to life by a poet who is S.P. to the life in his verse. The consequences of this event are difficult to foresee but it seems probable that it will give rise to second thoughts about S.P., D.Q. & C. and to certain modifications of established literary opinion; and this might be considered a good thing.

The titles of the two poems by Paul Vangelisti: 'MVCCLH' and 'Gof in Singapore' give the reader a clue as to how to read the two poems.

'MVCCLH' looks like Roman numerals – a date in Roman numerals – but is not.

We associate Roman numerals with the past, and under the title of the poem we read: 'The observer is the past.'

It is something Crazy Horse said and Crazy Horse we are bound to read as Crazy Horse *and* crazy horse; i.e., a horse gone crazy. These consequent and contradictory signals are structurally present in the 26 stanzas of the poem.

Even writing *lies* on the page.

We can think of the stanzas as the cards of a deck laid out on a table. Each card assumes a different meaning according to the game one is playing.

In the case of this poem it is the last verse of each stanza which gives the indication of the 'mood' the previous verses should be read in. The moods are varied and diverse – hopeful, deceived, desperate, descriptive, negative, barren, etc.

Some stanzas are very intense and explosive.

All the stanzas are what they are with the sole intention of making the reader aware of the reasons he is reading on.

The poet deals out the stanzas but is not present in the writing in the first person. Neither should the reader be in his reading.

'Gof in Singapore' is a typo. As such, it can be read: 'God in Singapore.'

As opposed to 'MVCCLH' which is an exercise in static dynamics, 'Gof in Singapore' leads to a definite climax.

The poet tries to hide in the folds of daily trivia but his first person acts like a magnet which attracts present and past biography and then expels it in exploded shrapnel.

The climax is: Gof of Singapore meets Marlene Dietrich on the Shanghai Express. The last line of the poem:

tomorrow he dreams of never having known you before

– *Giulia Niccolai*

John Thomas

from Patagonia

'... these desultory chapters, which might be described as a record of what I did not do...'

– W. H. Hudson, Idle Days in Patagonia

In Patagonia. An old house, deserted, its rooms choked with drifts of debris: broken chairs, stacks of mildewed books, old clothes and rat turds. Out in the dooryard weeds, a mattress, covered with ambiguous stains, leaks cotton batting. The wind is from the west and never stops.

When the days are warm enough, I choose a book at random from one of the many heaps and go out to lie on the mattress and read. In the west there are great snowy mountains, very picturesque. I rarely so much as glance at them. The wind never stops.

There is no temptation to hike into town. Town is three weeks away to the south. Would you walk that far just to be overcharged for a chilly room in a tin-roof hotel in Punta Arenas?

I had been telling my son Ezra how I loved Patagonia. How, all winter long, there was nothing to do but huddle in your blankets, drinking endless gourds of maté, listen to the wind howl overhead, and plan interesting ways of committing suicide. 'Jesus!' I said. 'How I love Patagonia!'

He had been growing visibly impatient. Finally he said, 'Well, then, why don't you just go, if you love it so much?'

'I'm *in* Patagonia,' I replied. He merely looked puzzled and irritated. We always disappoint one another thus, my son and I.

'The 7. day betweene the mouth of the Streights and the narrowest place thereof, wee tooke a Spaniard whose name was Hernando, who was there with 23 Spaniards more, which were all that remayned of foure hundred, which were left there three yeeres before in these streights of Magellan, all the rest being dead with famine. And the same day wee passed through the narrowest of the Streights, where the aforesayd Spanyard showed us the hull of a small Barke, which we judged to be a Barke called The John Thomas . . .'

– Hakluyt's *Voyages*

Only a hundred paces to the creek. No name to it, and I'm not about to give it one. The water flows swiftly most of the year, over big rocks, but you can't hear it, usually, until you are quite close: the wind, again. Steep banks – fossil oyster shells, many over a foot in diameter (Hatcher's oyster) – here and there the bones of animals (giant sloths? extinct camels?) poking out of the mud of the creek banks. Extinct penguins, some of them taller than a man.

There are supposed to be some graves up the creek, just around the bend on a little knoll on the near side. 'Worth checking out. Really. The only really interesting things in the area, outside of fossils.' A family plot, I suppose, containing the remains of former occupants of the house. Of course, I haven't 'checked them out.' I'm not here to visit points of local interest.

'Upon the highest part of the hilles **we found** some burying places, which were heapes of stones, and not **knowing** what that meant, pulled the stones off from one of them, and under them found men's bones of 10 and 11 foote long . . .'

– Willem Cornelison Schouten, 1615

The trash heap is in a little gully behind the house, on the way to the creek. On top of the heap, the skeleton of a small dog with patches of hide still clinging here and there. Grey-white fur with black spots. At the edge of the heap near the house, a man's brown lace-up knee boot. Run-over heel. He had very small feet. A slit at the side once accommodated a large bunion.

As a poet, upon my return (my daily, my hourly returns) from Patagonia, they would expect me to come bearing trophies. Poems. Well, fuck them and their expectations. Trophies. Anyway, what could I bring them? An old boot?

Poking in the trash heap. Seems he ate mostly bully beef, sardines, stuff like that. What did the dog eat? I haven't seen enough small animals around here to feed a dog, even a skillful hunter who (which? that? fuck it.) worked at it all day long. So what did he eat? Did he get his share of the canned beef? The two of them, sitting in the kitchen chomping away, wintertime maybe (August down here), two plates, one can, one fork, all the while this fucking wind?

'Twilight comes and brings an end to these useless researches; useless, I say, and I take great delight in saying it, for if there is anything one feels inclined to abhor in this placid land, it is the doctrine that all our investigations into nature are for some benefit, present or future, to the human race.'
                                                   – W. H. Hudson, *Idle Days in Patagonia.*

I still have nearly two cases of wine. Cheap *rosado* I bought nearly three months ago in Carmen de Patagones. The one-liter bottles are green plastic, in the shape of penguins. The empties I fill with dirt (to keep the wind from tipping them over); then I stand them up outside the kitchen door on the lee side of the house. Not everyone has a steadily-growing gang of penguins in his back yard. I have faced them all toward the skewed, open kitchen doorway. When I am drunk enough (and the wind permits), I sit on the stoop and tell them penguin jokes. They don't laugh, of course, but then, penguin jokes are not funny.

December 31. My birthday. Spent the day down by the creek in the bushes, picking montilla berries, or what the English in Patagonia call 'diddle-dee-dee.'

The Yaghan, Fuegian Indians extinct since the nineteenth century, defined 'monotony' as 'an absence of male friends.'

Books about Patagonia do not – cannot – have the traditional beginning, middle and end. They start at around page 350 and just peter out.

Patagonian autobiography, a model text: 'I was born, but . . .'

In Patagonia, to practice meditation is to bake mudpies in a toy stove.

In Patagonia, 'learning from one's mistakes' is much like eating those mudpies.

Not least among the advantages of a life in Patagonia ('the uttermost part of the earth') is the opportunity to die with some dignity. That is to say, there will be no doctors to interfere with me, and I shall be able to expire, in agony and perfect squalor, of some antique ailment conquered long since by medical science. The *prospect,* at least, amuses. Is this what I mean by 'penguin joke'?

The reader is now invited to peruse the forty-first chapter of *Moby Dick,* 'The Whiteness of the Whale.' Then, after a period given over to appropriate reflection, he is to imagine that I have inserted at this place in the text a curious parody of Melville's chapter. Think of it as evincing a subtle and oddly unsettling virtuosity. Call it, of course, 'The Greyness of Patagonia.'

'Now, I inquire, what impressions must be made upon the inhabitant of the Argentine Republic by the simple act of fixing his eyes upon the horizon and seeing nothing? – for the deeper his gaze sinks into that shifting, hazy, undefined horizon, the further it withdraws from him, the more it fascinates and confuses him, and plunges him in contemplation and doubt. What is the end of that world which he vainly seeks to penetrate? He knows not! What is there beyond what he sees? The wilderness, danger, the savage, death! Here is poetry already; he who moves among such scenes is assailed by fantastic doubts and fears, by dreams which possess his waking hours.'
– *Facundo: Life in the Argentine Republic in the Days of the Tyrants;*
or, Civilization and Barbarism, by Domingo F. Sarmiento

Rosado all gone, and my regiment of penguins has reached its full complement. They have (after a spiritless debate) elected me their hetman or coronel. Now, unless I want to hike to Punta Arenas, it's maté, marijuana and cough medicine for me.

THE DANCE OF THE PENGUINS

they
don't
dance

Back in California there are several women, a pair of fifteen-year-old Chicana twins, and even a lad of twelve, who would be mightily surprised – mortified, even – to learn how often and in what eccentric combinations they had had sex with me on a lumpy mattress in the weeds outside a collapsing house in Patagonia. Perhaps, though, at night they hear the wind howling in their dreams of penguins?

April 30th. 'Camerone.' Traditional holiday of the Foreign Legion. On this day in Mexico in 1863 a small Legion company, commanded by an elderly Spanish captain with a glass eye and a wooden arm, fought to the death at the Hacienda de Camerone to cover the retreat of French forces to Vera Cruz.

This morning, by way of celebration, I organized a little defeat for myself. Dug into my knapsack and found the unlabeled pill bottle I'd been saving. Seven shiny yellow tablets, old now and turning a mottled brown. Don't remember what they are. Were. Took them with my morning maté. Half an hour later I was sitting on the kitchen step, singing Legion songs to my demibrigade of penguins. '*Tiens, voilà du boudin. . . .*' '*Je ne regrette rien.*' On and on, until my voice broke and I withdrew into the house, weeping in a transport of self-pity. I felt the scissors of Atropos nibbling at my thread. My faculties were, as they say, under a cloud.

I was awakened late in the afternoon (in the front yard – what was I doing there?) by the sting of hail on my cheeks, lips, eyelids. The day's rain had turned into the first hailstorm of the year. Shivering, I rolled off the soaked mattress and crawled back to the house.

My copybook lay open on the kitchen table. I had been writing, it would appear, during the lost hours. Peered at the scrawled notes. Ah, shit, more prefaces. First page, just banalities:

Fragments of a work in progress. [illegible] of failure. Negative transcendence. Progress as cliché. Or as the oncologist might, each morning, gaze [into his?] shaving mirror and contemplate the 'progress' of his own melanoma. ('The Man with the Flower in His Mouth,' but with a sly shift of emphasis.) Or progress as vegetable decay: the rotten tree stump that glows in the dark.

I lick my finger, turn the page. Just more of the same. But as old Father Guzmán wrote in 1837 (I translate roughly from his elegant Latin): 'Being in Patagonia without a reason . . . would imply a mental condition to which no one would confess.'

Most writers would regard Southern California as banishment enough. To live in Los Angeles, a minor poet of some local repute: surely this satisfies any interpretation of the Doctrine of Sufficient Disgrace. Well, for me, nothing has ever proved Sufficient. The Fatal Flaw, amigo.

I have cast my ballot with Plato's, albeit for different reasons. Scratched my own poor name on the *óstrakon*. Voted myself right out of the Republic.

So. And there must be no stopping at Harrar. Because – follow the argument where it leads, through a jumble of metaphor – because even in Harrar the Person from Porlock knocks every day, the perfect excuse.

I do get visitors now and then, as you will see, but never from Porlock. In Patagonia there are no excuses.

Notebook jottings – failed attempts to characterize this book for A Lady:

1. 'Scenes of Provincial Life.'
2. 'Oblomov in Patagonia.'
3. 'Satyricon' = *satura / saturika* = 'a potpourri or farrago of mixed subjects in a variety of styles' / 'concerned with satyrs, i.e. lecherous, randy.'

4. And/or 'Zuihitsu' – that is to say, random jottings as a literary form. As Kenkō put it, in the 14th century, 'Leisurely I face my inkstone all day long, and without any particular object jot down the odds and ends that pass through my mind, with a curious feeling that I am not sane.'

Reading, writing, self-pollution, drugs and sleep: these are the five great depravities of solitude. But from time to time, even for me, the taste for private squalor can lose its keenness of edge. About once a month The Great World calls. A little *pasear,* that's the ticket. So I button my fly, put on my boots, and sally forth into society.

East for eight miles on the dirt track which parallels the creek. The wind is at my back, raving, shoving me rudely along. South, then, on the highway, staggering sometimes, leaning to my right so as not to be blown clear off the road. But I soldier on. Two more miles of gravel, mud and potholes bring me to my nearest neighbor, Celedonio Ramos.

Celedonio Ramos. An Asturian, he says. He lives here with his hare-lipped daughter Escolástica. Boliche Las Pulgas, he calls his place. A *boliche* is a sort of barroom and country store. *Las pulgas* means 'the fleas.'

Harness on the walls. Dusty canned goods on a few dusty shelves. A drum of kerosene in a corner. The bar. Its shelf, behind, with bottles of Mendoza brandy, *rosado,* some sweet vermouth. Faded poster above the shelf: CINZANO–AMERICANO GANCIA. No customers. My neighbor and his fortyish daughter sit at the bar over a late lunch.

'Don Celedonio, how goes it? Señorita Escolástica?'

Celedonio extends his thick paw in the soft and furtive handshake of this region. Escolástica grants me a ghastly, split-faced simper, says something. It is a hopeless gobble, but interrogatory. My grin congeals and I look rather wildly to Celedonio for help.

'She says you look hungry. She invites you to join us at our repast. I also invite you. She says something else, which is lost. There are limits of comprehension even for me, her father. Come and sit with us. There is plenty.'

The meal consists of boiled sheep's head and soggy fried bread. Room is made for me and I belly up to the counter. Escolástica serves me with her own hand, heaping my plate with tidbits: morsels of cheek-meat, half a greyish tongue, thick cuts of bread.

We take our time. Don Celedonio pours the wine, waving away my pesos, but allows me to pay for postprandial drinks. We two men nurse our brandy: the day will be a long one. The lady snuffles a sweet vermouth, her face the face of a camel. And how do we while away our afternoon? As Don Celedonio puts it, we 'listen to the trucks.'

Like the afternoon itself, the road stretches past the *boliche*: grey, dusty and trafficless. 'Listening to the trucks.' There are no trucks, of course. Oh, sometimes we hear a truck; we know it surely is a truck, but it is the wind. Or the noise of gears changing down, but that also is the wind. Sometimes the wind sounds like an unloaded truck banging over a timber bridge.

We look up the road, see a dust-devil, think it's a truck. Or there are black specks that seem to be coming closer, and we are certain at last that this is both a car and a truck. But the specks walk off sideways, and we realize they were sheep.

Finally, near sundown, when we no longer believe, comes a truck. Dusty old 2½-ton Dodge, painted park-bench green. It bumps slowly south along the track. Two beeps of the horn as it passes. On the door, in yellow paint: SOUTH SEA TRUCKING. On the tailgate, in orange: MAMA, LOOK AT ME NOW!!

The truck sways off, bound for Río Gallegos and the Straits. The sob of its engine is swallowed up in the wind that sounds like trucks.

Door and window are both shut tight, but the air inside Las Pulgas is heavy with salty wind-blown grit. Several times during the afternoon, Escolástica excuses herself and crosses the room to dust her lithographs.

Highly-colored German prints, two of them, hanging on the wall opposite the bar. I remember having seen them in Bolivia, Peru, Ecuador and Colombia, and in one or two Mexican saloons.

'The Sleeping Hunters': Three plump fellows, dressed in odd green uniforms, wearing gaiters and tiny Tyrolean hats with brushes of chamois hair stuck into them. The men are fast asleep beneath a tree with bluish-green foliage. They seem to be resting after a hearty meal: near them lie the remains of food and several empty bottles. A stag and two does sniff the shotguns which stand propped up against the tree-trunk, and rabbits help themselves to bread. This is a sort of masterpiece, and with an idea behind it – not to mention its technical virtues, its composition and super-imaginative coloring.

'Russian Winter': An expanse of white snow, a sleigh being attacked by a pack of wolves, horses galloping madly, men shooting in every direction, two of the slavering beasts rolling over, staining the snow with bright red blood. This amazing picture projects an atmosphere of intense cold, and at the same time the spiritual sensation of heat.

From the bar, we watch her as she attacks the prints with brisk flicks of her feather duster.

'These works of art – they are her solace,' Don Celedonio remarks phlegmatically, then speaks no more about it. (Here in Patagonia, you see, the chronic lust for solace is taken for granted. Only the instruments of solace, or its palliatives, seem worthy of remark.)

Escolástica's feather duster: it is one of those souvenir dusters from Comodoro Rivadavia, made of ostrich feathers (Darwin's rhea) that had been shipped from Comodoro to Germany, there simply fastened to sticks, and then shipped back again.

Y al campo me iba solito,
más matrero que el vanao,
como perro abandonao,
a buscar una tapera,
o en alguna biscachera
pasar la noche tirao.
(*And I'd go off all alone to the plains,/ sneakier than a deer,/ like a stray dog,/ to look for a ruined shack/ to shelter in, or to pass the night/ stretched out in a viscacha-warren.*)

– stanza 1430, 'El Gaucho Martín Fierro,'
by José Hernández

Five whole days in Punta Arenas with Lili and Raquel, sisters, from Chiloé, Jehovah's Witnesses. No actual fucking allowed, but they have some very odd ideas about what *is* allowed. Raquel, it seems, is in direct daily communication with the Paraclete, Who (Which?) is giving us (through her) secret sexual instruction. Esoteric doctrine it is, not to be passed on even to other Witnesses. The Time Is Not Yet Ripe, don't you know?

Lili sneaks tracts into my duffel. One of them I have kept. I read it to my penguins often:

THE ONE AND ONLY FRIEND OF MAN
(the one who bears him no rancor)
True missionaries assume the authority and concentration of the Apostle Paul.

No sociology without salvation
No political economy without the Evangelist
No reform without redemption
No culture without conversion
No progresss without forgiveness
No new social order without a new birth
No new organization without a New Creation
No democracy without the Divine Word
NO CIVILIZATION WITHOUT CHRIST
ARE WE READY TO DO WHAT OUR MASTER ORDERS (according to his express desires)

'... now I suck Raquel until she scream and shake all over and make pipi.' Which she did, and Raquel did most copiously. And the three of us later under the smelly blankets, listening to the wind, telling ghost stories. The girls tell me of Chiloé, sing (badly) Chilote songs, weep. Raquel sits on her heel, masturbating, while I sodomize Lili. Lili starts to come, speaks in tongues.

Later, Lili describes her colonic raptures as something very like a large bird that churns her tripes with great and softly-fluttering wings. Raquel assumes an omniscient smirk. 'Of course it is a bird,' she says. 'It is a dove. *La Paloma*. The Holy Spirit, as is well known, frequently assumes that form. Matthew 3 : 16.'

Lili is suitably impressed. 'Yes, surely,' she sighs. 'A dove, with great wings. And a sharp beak. Let us pray.'

I bow my head and close my eyes out of respect for my darlings' devotions, but I should tell you that I have grave doubts. I rather think it was a penguin.

Both Lili and Raquel have a bottomless appetite for ghost stories. By now I have told them all I recall, however imperfectly, from my childhood reading: Poe, Lovecraft, Algernon Blackwood, etc. Their particular favorite is 'The Golden Arm,' told as Mark Twain said it should be told. Even more to their taste are my narrative renderings of American monster movies of the 1930s and 1940s.

Lili's identification with the victims is sharp and immediate, and she sinks easily into a voluptuous trance of child-like dread. Raquel's sympathies, as you might suppose, lie elsewhere. With each fresh atrocity 'her nostrils flare and her proud eyes flash fire.'* At the end, when the mummy is twisting in agony, trapped in a bloom of fire, his tattered linen cerements ablaze, Raquel sits erect on the bed, her eyes tear-filled but still proud.

'He will return,' she whispers.

Lili, quaking, buried under the blankets, begins to moan at the prospect.

The talk turns to 'real' mummies. I tell them that the museums of the world have rooms full of them. Lili peeps silently out at me, her eyes great pools of delighted horror.

'Rooms filled with *momias,* you say?' marvels Raquel. 'To be approached and seen? You yourself have been in such a room?'

I assure her that I have.

'How fine a thing that must have been! I yearn to go there one day!'

Lili is not so sure. Being a Jehovah's Witness, she lives in constant daily expectation of the end of the world. Well, she challenges, what if one were in such a place at The Great Moment? What if the General Resurrection occurred even as one stood among those solemn corpses turned into a sight for sightseers?

'They would stand up, you see, and stagger about. I would go mad with my terror!' And she pops under the blankets again.

Raquel caresses her gently.

'Do not be afraid,' she soothes. 'Such a thing would not happen. I, your sister, have been promised two days' special warning of the Second Coming.'

No doubt she has. She always seems to know, even before I do, when I am about to come.

* E. P. Roe, *What Can She Do?*, p. 157.

The privy is out of sight of the house, past the trash heap in a natural hollow. It is of wooden planks buttressed on three sides by heaped stones. It has been left well-supplied with stacks of sanitary literature.

There are the usual illustrated magazines from Buenos Aires. Eva Perón's smooth and smiling face appears on most of their covers. Today I read a most interesting and instructive account of the death of a famous singer and composer of tangos, cut off at the peak of his career in a fiery plane crash somewhere up in the Gran Chaco. There is a fine catalog of saddlery, which I hope to save. I know most of the pictures by heart, as well as the prices of spurs, whips, lassos, and many other items in the long list.

Scrawled on the inside of the privy door with a thick blunt pencil that dug deeply into the wood: 'Nobiembre 7 de 1935 dejó de existir Metet por mano de Segundo.' ('On the 7th of November, 1935, Metet ceased to exist, by the hand of Segundo.')

Eva Perón, in Argentine folk tradition, has long ranked with Cleopatra as one of the great fellatrices in world history. So naturally, from time to time, sitting in the privy, I have stroked my penis while pondering Eva's bland sly face on a warped and faded magazine page. But it has never worked for me. On the contrary, the idea of entrusting my member to that mouth, to those historic lips, has always left me uneasy and limp.

No. For me, fame and skill don't seem to work. I prefer my two little missionaries from Chiloé. They are so inept, each in her own fashion, that they never fail to charm and arouse me.

Lili is all shivering urgency and sweet confusion. She moans and mumbles, chokes and murmurs. Her greed makes her clumsy: at the end she will be coughing and snuffling in frustration, with semen running from her nostrils, dripping from her chin into her cupped and trembling palm.

Raquel, on the other hand, is all technique. Perhaps another personal revelation from Him: I've never asked. She assumes an expression of quiet and mysterious competence, clasps my member in a fashion that suggests the handgrip of some obscure secret society, and commences to nibble. From beginning to end, she does it all wrong, with an almost patronizing confidence and serenity. The air is thick with pathos, naïveté. She is so . . . quaint. She so utterly misses the point that I never fail to grow excited. She munches and sucks until the first spurt of semen has filled her mouth; then she prefers to sit back and pump my staff with her fist, gazing triumphantly at the glistening sperm as it trickles down over her knuckles. Eva simply isn't in the running.

'After the mule comes nothing.' It is obvious that Gauguin was never in Patagonia.

'Oh, Herbert, let's go,' Marjorie exclaimed.

Without waiting for an answer, she pirouetted about the room singing: 'We're going to Patagonia! We're going to Patagonia!'

I suggested that she read the 'enclosure' with its strange South American heading. . . .

– from *El Jimmy, Outlaw of Patagonia,*
by Herbert Childs

Punta Arenas. A cold black late afternoon in July. The wind roars outside. Hail drums on the tin roof. In my hotel room, Lili, Raquel and I crouch on straight chairs in a semi-circle around the muttering oil stove. I wear my long johns, an old Argentine military overcoat, and three of the hotel's musty blankets. The girls are naked under heavy, greasy wool ponchos. The air in the room smells of kerosene, dirty wool, armpits and recent sex. Are we happy? Plenty of codeine and maté, and the stove works, so the question never presents itself.

Desultory conversation. The maté gourd passes from hand to hand. Raquel is the *cebador* (the maker, or server, of maté). She brews it, spits out the bitter first gourdful, then brews the second and passes it to the left to me. I drink it and pass back the gourd. The third brew goes to Lili, and so on. When the water no longer foams, Raquel dumps out the yerba and starts again. It is Lili's task to clean the bombilla when it clogs.

The codeine has made me garrulous, and I have been trying to explain why I no longer write poems.

'Oh, they still come to me,' I say. 'Sometimes they drop into my head perfect and complete. Good poems, too.' (I am lollygagging, as I have said.) 'But then when it comes to writing them down, a part of me says 'NO!' And I don't. And that refusal, *caras,* brings with it a pleasure far sharper than anything I've felt when merely writing.'

Raquel grins, but Lili looks angry and perplexed. *'¡Pucha!'* she says at last. *'¡Embromador!* For shit sure you lying us now!'

'No, it's true. I don't understand it, but the pleasure is there. I've told other poets, and they doubt me, too.'

She frowns and shrugs under her poncho.

'But I, I understand,' says Raquel.

'Do you?'

'Oh, yes. And I will do you the parable of it. You will see.'

Dropping to her knees beside me, she pushes blankets and overcoat aside and fishes my penis out of my underwear. It promptly shrivels in the cold. She glares at it sternly.

'Listen!' she commands. 'You must be the hard thing for my parable. So . . .' (shaking a schoolmistressy finger at it) 'be hard!'

I laugh, but once again her idiotic self-assurance wins out: to my amazement, up it stands – and bobs in polite attention.

'Now, Sister,' she says, gesturing to Lili. 'Come down here. Make a pussy with your fist. Do with it what pussies do.'

While Lili jerks me off, Raquel fetches one of my boots from beside the bed. She unlaces it and ties the lace around the base of my cock in a loose overhand knot.

'Do not stop, Sister, until I tell you.'

Lili nods, puzzled but obedient. Raquel fixes her gaze on my scrotum. Sooner than I would have supposed, Lili's fingers accomplish their task and I start to come. My scrotum contracts.

'Now!' hisses Raquel. 'No poems!'

She pulls the knotted shoelace tight. My urethra collapses. I come, flopping like a caught fish. For a moment, I black out.

When my vision clears, Lili is still chafing my penis – which is still stiff and growing purple.

'Okay, Sister, now you stop.'

Lili shows us her trembling hand. No semen. And none on my cock.

'¡Ay!' she breathes. '¡Pero es un crimen!' ('Oh, but that is a crime!')

Raquel is smiling. 'Not a crime,' she says. 'A parable.'

Carefully she loosens the knot. Freed, my cock droops and the semen pours slowly into her cupped palm. I stare, bemused. After a solemn interval, she raises her hand, first to Lili's lips and then to her own, and her 'parable' is finished.

She is crazy, my Raquel, mad as a hatter. No argument there. That is why I am unnerved to find that she understands me so well.

And so we sit, late into the night. Maté and codeine and more maté, while the wind raves outside. 'The uttermost part of the earth.'

In the morning, the maid comes into my room at a most awkward moment. She is horrified by what she sees. We have been . . . well, no matter. The speechless girl stands staring and crossing herself. Raquel leaps up. She is clad only in my black vest and her hair is all snakes. Brandishing her big bible, she drives the maid from the room, then shouts abuse at her in twittering Chilean as she flees down the hall.

The little concierge avoids my eyes while asking me to leave.

'You understand, sir. We are men of the world, you and I, but I cannot afford the scandal of it. And the maid: she is from the nuns, you see. The orphanage. She is still not herself.'

We listen, he and I. She is sobbing hysterically behind the office door.

'It's all right,' I say. 'I understand.'

'And those girls, sir. They are . . . *evangelistas?* Missionaries? How can this be?'

'Well . . . '

'You will, of course, take them with you.'

Not enough money for another hotel, so we spend the day shivering on street corners. I panhandle, with little success. For a while, Lili and Raquel pass out tracts. Then they produce tambourines ('RECUERDO DE PUERTO MONTT' painted on the skins) and sing hymns. The wind whips their thin voices away, and the vapor-clouds of their breath.

By mid-afternoon there is sleet again and it is pitch dark, just little pools of light under the street lamps. We huddle together in a doorway, count our money, plan our last evening in Punta Arenas.

Four blocks at a clumsy run, leaning into the wind, sleet stinging our faces, to the Turkish bath. Valdivia 999, corner of O'Higgins. For two pesos I am given soap, towel and a cardboard comb – they the same, I suppose, on the ladies' side. We meet afterwards in the vestibule and cut out running again. We'll sit in the town cinema until closing time.

'The Cervantes theatre,' says the *South American Handbook,* 'is so ornate it is worth buying a cinema ticket to see it; the films shown are old.'

Tonight: 'The Cid,' Charlton Heston and Sophia Loren, dubbed in Spanish. Old, yes, but popular here. It has been playing for thirteen weeks. Lili and Raquel tell me they have already seen it twenty-eight times.

And the *Handbook* has not lied about the theatre itself. It is an infected improvisation on a theme of Piranesi, built by a demented pastry chef. The girls are licking ice cream cones. Bought them in the lobby. Tiny things and very narrow, topped with little dollops of something magenta. Vile-looking. I tell them that in 1928 my father invented the double-header. This is hard to say in Spanish.

Lili is shocked. 'With two heads? Such a deformity!'

'A *capricho*,' Raquel explains. 'For the Day of the Dead. Something *macabro* to terrify the children.'

'No, no.' I revise. 'A cone, like these, but with two cups at the top. Side by side, to hold more ice cream.'

Lili still looks puzzled, so Raquel explains once more.

'*Claro*, sister. Like all barbarians, *Yanquis* are very greedy. They must have two of all things.'

I try again to clear things up, but Lili shushes me.

'He comes!' she whispers.

And Charlton Heston's head fills the screen. Squinty little eyes, skewed blade of a nose, a tight-fitting hood of plastic chain mail.

'He comes!' She points him out to me, cone in her fist like a broken scepter. Her other hand disappears under her skirt. In the dimness, I catch Raquel's eye. She shrugs, smiles indulgently.

'I always wait for *Señora* Loren. You must wait with me. By then I am finished to eat this cone of one head and I shall pollute me and you also. You will see how it will be better.'

Who am I to question her? She's watching the film for the twenty-ninth time, so she's the expert.

In the lobby, two complete shows later, we are all three haggard and sleepy. Yawns, muted farewells. (The girls will sleep in some sort of hospice, non-Witnesses not admitted.) Raquel pats my cheek; Lili tucks a tract into my overcoat pocket.

Okay. North along the coast tomorrow, but tonight it's the Salvation Army for me. Calle Bella Vista 377. For 50¢ U.S., they let you sleep on the floor at the back of the hall.

But the floor is too cold, the hail on the tin roof too loud. I spend most of the long austral night in the lavatory, reading old copies of the *Magellan Times*. English-language paper, mostly sheep prices and shipping news. When I look up to stare at my reflection in the mirror over the sinks, I see cloud shapes and flickering flames.

Fifty-three degrees south latitude and sinking.

My penguins have a favorite story. It really has no name, but they call it 'Riding North in Other People's Cars.' I must tell it to them at least once a week, and it goes like this:

'Punta Arenas, Río Verde, San Gregorio, Punta Delgada . . . '

'Next comes the border!' cry the penguins.

'Right, next comes the border. And then?'

'Monte Aymond!'

'Yes! And then?'

'Río Gallegos! A hundred and fifty miles!'

'Coy Aike, Puerto Coig, Cañadon de las Vacas, Monte León . . . '

'Comandante Luis Piedrabuena!' Many squawks and cheers.

'Santa Cruz, Río Chico, San Julián, El Salado, La Porteña . . . ah, Tellier?'

'No, no! Puerto Deseado!' (They know that *I* know, but they love to correct me.)

'Oh, right. Puerto Deseado, *then* Tellier. Then Antonio de Biedma, Cerro Blanco. Las Martinetas, Jaramillo, FitzRoy, Pico . . . ah, Pico . . . '

'Pico Truncado!'

'Of course. Truncado. Cañadon Seco . . . '

'Getting close!' they cry, interrupting me, always at this point.

'Caleta Olivia.'

'Closer!'

'Holdich!' *I'm* yelling, now. And we end it all together.

'CO-MO-DO-RO RI-VA-DA-VI-AAAAAA!'

Much cheering and general hilarity.

Back here in Los Angeles, if I am depressed, I can always raise my spirits by muttering to myself, 'Comodoro Rivadavia!' At night I can whisper, 'Comodoro Rivadavia!' and fall swiftly to sleep and always dream of penguins.

'Yet, in passing over these scenes, without one bright object near, an ill-defined but strong sense of pleasure is vividly excited.'
                                    – Charles Darwin, *The Voyage of the Beagle*

(*to be continued*)

Robert Crosson

Wet Check

'wet check': money paid a player for damage to personal wardrobe or for personal discomfort, hardship and/or hazard, in the course of his/her employment as player.

— Screen Extras Guild

The Great Bronze Age of China

first of all 2 dimes in yr pocket
wall-pictures of mines they dug
the treasures out calendars pitted
green pots & wine jugs under plexi-
glass made chinese brunch

*

rude girls with radios in their ear
cast bronze shadows inlaid with copper
& ivory skin noted they must in their
prime have been polished ceremonials
that sacrifice

*

feathers on the stairs
stone warriors propped up with their
horses rode stone follicles for hair
a jade phallus bridled & pitched
forward

'which accounts for their stance

*

poolside
with bobbed tails

*

swum.

Video

    Beatrice pounds clay
    Beatrice fashions lines of blood
    across the palm she descends
    nude upon

    Beatrice mounts sermons
    Beatrice entertains
    Beatrice began her day
    before lunch and the photographers
    came

Beatrice did not know Dante
(barely introduced to him)

    them Egyptian barges upon the
    slumbering Styx
          sd Beatrice:
          'Tediously sensible, that man
          and no fun.'

    Gave rise to prophetic rocks
    exploded dust whole towns
    had to abandon
          Helena erupts.
          (wagner over)

       ★

       'Straw make the best picnic,'
       she daresay
    Hymen presides.
       'Most bauble with mouths agape'
       she thought with.
    Does.
    They do.
    'one room crowded with very large
    & very ugly furniture occasionally
    shifted to redecorate

       and not an aisle
       to walk in.'

In the end, they marry
    (after that, three false endings where one wd have done
        thumping punctuations the piece ws finished
    the throne restored
    good kings to their cousins

go out, play some poker, get their mind off things)
the forest real, flesh likewise.
Tears dried.

    boy Rosalynd gets her man.

        ★

      The ragwoman – cats dead she talks to
          oilwells beneath the city
     'Don't get too well-known,
look what happened to Lindbergh.'

      drumbeats

Horse

1

'why did you die?' he sd

---

the truth facsimile he saved 3 bottlecaps for
then led to water

i have no idea why pots boil why
lights go out

'man is only good as his horse'

'i did not know that' he sd

lips & tongue & such pretty white teeth)
he tethered
   bareback
      lady godiva

& clippered toenails
possibly)

---

ded he is not
      for mouths sake

for blind boulders for
rock the high ridge
ranched up there

(that pass

'the orderly way is to post fences
& paint them white to stake yr grass
clover'

• • •

close-up: lips &
tongue (articulating

the plosive dental
the bedside labial
rung yellow as the insides of trees
years account ded reckoning

            'one look in the mouth' he sd
            (tidy, that sound of it

& lugged the mails for wells fargo
cantering sweat, trotted new routes
to mexico

2

'long in the tooth'
being heartbeat
made invention

'narrowing it down'
    the pencil upright
    poised for the picket

    ★

'horses got to have good eyes'

            to get at the apple
            the oats you put
            under my nose

                'i will ride you' (he sd

i will hound you out
i will take yr name
            that cold shower you neither laugh nor beckon
            just bridle, shivering
there will come a day
when that calmly i am not afraid of you
them words you don't have

that busyiness & wd stay so
reckless.

mails must go out
there far west

            i wd

cantankerously
(& know that

        •

                'give a guy a break' he sez

even though my leg hurts
that makes me laugh

3
dear sir:
this is to inform you that horses can be trained
i am an expert in this matter when i am running
i can stop as i do occasionally i do not care
who watches from

the earth is not round it is pear shaped
on good days i gallop

great thoughts i have (which does alarm most
ded in my tracks
i do not know how i got here transported

by land
upon bridges
perhaps

i can be tot to do most anything

sincerely yrs

ps.

wasnt tom mix planted my foot at graumans
chinese theâter.

The Fastest Gun in the West

o yes that
catholic god
wits & witness

palm trees doheny
before the sunset
orange groves &
hill barren
free to be (bought)
picture postcards

the story ws
this a house a dog
trying to get in
goblins geese
losing weight make
test of virility a
cornucopia of slick
shells one goose
a guinea hen

'my dear we have been here before'
two sides holding a doorknob
smarting a first dose of crabs
the dog human (as sheets go) 3 $
extra to shower in rooms shared
the hollywood address
hirsute (suite) palms
on franklin avenue

first it was captain marvel
encumbrances sunk the ship in
voices dittering offstage
'that horse cant be rode'
but by god i did it 5
times around on my ass
the first take &
without glasses
caught the bag of gold

★

coffee shop.
this guy comes in

deaf jack from the old
boarding-house days 15
yrs since hes seen me
'you still in the acting game?'
one night modelling a tiger-girl
in suit jack takes pictures with
his color polaroid

star to the territory

catcalls (off) the
proscenium arch
snorting by-yr-leaves

★

'global to be sure'

that moat & fortress
held drawbridge she
took back roads from
life (or film) held
terror to

'my dear we live here'

backstage lots
abandoned
properties

'extras are not people
      bits should associate with'

            ★

      you knock the lamp over
      that is good luck
      one goose dead
      & i open in
      2 weeks.
      today
      i buried it

she sd i was a genius i
believed her i cd fly when
i wanted i cd mount walls
verily and do

cyclopean steps
up the outside
rock amphitheater

★

guns are for people to shoot with
i found that out when i ws in the
war guns are heroes & guns make
heroes stronger i stand for that
guns are war, can warn off the
gas company or mad dogs up the hill
say coyotes

            tin targets of an evening
when i am john wayne & intend to be

            ★   ★   ★   ★

listen i have a very good vocabulary to tell you
the truth i can screw you without yr knowing it
& love you for it i am no star-fucker that is a
lie i ws put on this stage to say god made me
special i ws born with it you can keep philosophy
ill take shakespeare theater is my life it runs
in the family

★   ★   ★

i am very loving
until someone shoots my guinea hen
or turns out to be a drunk i do not
like drunks they fuck up i speak
from experience the real man walks
in his own boots i do not drink or
smoke i am a vegetarian.

so i ws born with a silver spoon
call me a playboy in this life
you use everything you have

        im running aboard ship
        the total holocaust i
        did my own stuntwork
        (scale) 'in water this
        deep and no wet check

        'horses i can handle
        but that

            the supply clerk
        celebrated home during
        the mud slide
        george sand

telling about gray rains
in mallorca the piano
peasants so troublesome

'got medals to prove it'

        ★

i dont doubt it
given half the chance
id shoot the sonsabitches down myself

a sure draw from the hip (target
that guitar hanging poolside)
and take the fuckers in 6 fast shots
like that
12 blocks south of the company store
yr legs thumping
to run a fast bum check

        ★

        star shop
        picture postcards

        okay so i ws captain marvel
        i ws also batman & wore a cape
        i still have, wear boxingmitts
        with my sandrock padded dummy-bag
        my goat stands audience

fuck the neighbors
i am my own man my mother made me
i demand the best that is tickets
paid for this is war to yr friend
be faithful i did not
strangle my wife

   ★

she just lost her brother
she is a champion skater
she can hit hard she ripped
the doorjamb off & threatened
the hinges that is some lady
(she also painted my bedroom silver)
i asked her which brother she ws calling
'the dead one,' she sd

thats on my telephone bill

Rockford

Nov. 1

Handed in hand exterior and deliberate
dictum
Immer
the elegy.
Elegy watch. Elgin place.
destination bed slept
decapitated
blood everywhere
Elgin.
pulsating nouns surrounding that
slow-motion leap that leaded glass
somebody put their ass through
them voices they talk at

— TV : *Election Debates*

★ ★ ★

THE CLUB

To the twilight of the rich
the benefaction,
to the poor
the wonder.

Sunday Nov. 2

A view of LACE from the Los Angeles Times Building :

LACE NEEDS YOUR SUPPORT

Indeed, yes.
Everywhere

and hurrah.

Dear Ania :
The cabinet is built and delivered. Leslie
helped ($10) − 58 × 32. I rested it on Cady's blanket
in my car.
Disparities apply : tac rags need foil, the house
is full of sawdust and wood shavings . . . The smell of
lacquer will vanish . . . An airplane sputters overhead,
the geese honk ; the hand turns to where the heart is.
I just got paid . . .

Nov. 3

Ania:

Reagan and Carter rally for the race. My checks
are covered. Today I got a credit card from the phone
company in the mail . . . no word as yet from New York.
No news anywhere except the fire in Laurel Canyon, a
dead dog no one can find, and sundry dryrot personal
re-evaluations that make me monstrous to myself and
unfit company for anyone. Earthworms do not have fun.
I do not send boxes of fall leaves; and have avoided
all baptisms. I prefer the short visit . . . Louva Jesson
has given me two bags of Ralph's jockey-shorts, size
42: they look brand-new. I do not believe in conversa-
tions. period. Grandeur I lack.

I will make a pot of stew, maybe watch television.

– 7/30 pm
daylightsavings

Halloween, I slept on the porch.

★　★　★　★

TV : *YELLOW ROSE CAFE*

'He's a perfect idiot.'

FLO :
Should be, he's spent a lifetime working at it.

★　★　★　★

A perfectionist is one who spends
too much time rehearsing failure.
This makes him competent: a respect-
ful audience to plump watermelon
& the daily accident.

1/am

Dere Rockford:

Ania says she likes my handwriting 'unstudied';
not the precise order and shape, but the struggle to
keep the line straight . . .
I am all postures then. Today a variation that draws
continuity the same task the hand makes. The hand.
Sandpaper.

Just dropped my cigarette. . . .

Start again: 3/45 am
(crickets trill)

a dark thicket

the celebrant is not

[42]

(litigious)
these.
This. If I stop
you would. You see

    rooms for rent.
I don't want to

        Nov. 4

Rockford:

    You expect me to tell you what you already know.
That is best done in conversation, a ritual comfort
I find worst enemy. Toys are marketed; grand truths
are margarine... So you went to school with Reagan's
brother: I bear left. My shoulder is weak from nerves
the muscles won't tone to, & have trouble lifting
barrels...
    You can't be a magician when your seams show, the
trick is to do it well and hide the obvious.

        ★

    (6/20 am)
    I am quitting early.

decadent: 19th cent.
Fr. and Eng.: 'abnormal
subject; subtilized style'
    – re Pasolini.

• • •

7/am

    lights blossom
    lemon fog turns mast
    seaward

    •

    chairs change points

    •

    dry (edibles)

        via *PV.*

gossip:
companion, crony

Sunday Nov. 9

    To Ania's: saw off doors, install peg-
    board. Ania phones Hagen – (poetry: Meister,
    Petrarca Preis)

closed windows beyond the kitchen sink

•

ledge with three green tomatoes

•

bicycle behind the blindless glass

•

blue mailbox at the corner

Ania :

Wash windows at Simon's.
Put last coat of varathane on finished cabinet.
(The glass louvres, I punch in with a rubber mallet.
Dog Rusty barks.

• • •

'Dry bones can harm no one!'

11/pm
(preludes)

★
★
★

'Halcyon'

however she stood she was loud a large woman
generous and noisily proud of minor accomp-
lishment let us say a southern anthem her
stance would betray in rooms too small for
her spirit she

•

a decadent youth succumbs to tables set for
six in candlelight the wit of courtesy made
numb in half the time it took to play the
minute waltz at the keyboard (there were
people who lived with maids & outspoken
retainers rich drapes white rugs you could
not hear yr feet in

•

was a cheerleader in her youth who on one
high occasion one cd certainly hear it
married well and danced across the sporting
field in nothing but long underwear; after-
wards she wrote a poem for the new yorker
(strident she sd, my metaphor: a woman stalk-
ing through mans legs), & one i read about a
chinaberry tree

•

a cottage house she made celebrity and for my
housewarming wd have hired an accordionist

•

she laughed she drank she liked to dance (no
recital at high tea fondly classical: an enter-
tainment of oval windows & meticulously manicured
front lawns she wd have no part of) – she ws a
rebel: i supposed that ws why she'd befriended
me (an egregious error i avoided by hiding on
the roof

― end, *Arabian Nights.*

Nov. 10

Ania:

The matter is not yet settled. I am still working
on it. The dishes are washed, I did that last night.
An hour's rain today, I hauled the rolled rug inside
from the porch. That is my new carpet which like me has
yet to be laid. All in due time, there are factors at
work. We must proceed cautiously.
God? you say ...
I agree with Thomas:
it's two guys running it: in Trenton.
Two Greeks, brothers, who live above a candy store.
One is in a wheelchair.

•   •   •   •

Oct. 5

Rockford:

Our case lies in the clock. The clock and the
calendar are everything. When nothing is counted we
can do what we want. Sawdust sits – grunting sideways
to tie my shoes I have sat in it.
Two cigarettes left. Gottschalk Oscar Peterson Kate
Smith & Johann Sebastian ... I've had to turn the
phonograph down. My nextdoor neighbor insists on
feeding his barnyard. He shoots BB's at my tin tub.
My refrigerator is still running: it makes surly
noises in the night.

P.S. The name is *Velda Carrots* ...
The anonymous lady on the telephone suggested
the name was *Carrosh:* it is Carrots. She is a
pleasant, electric lady who likes young men,
regularly hides her bottle, and prefers sherry.
I have to put doors on the cabinet by tomorrow.
I do not trust your advice about the hinges.
The damned sawdust is everywhere.

[45]

Oct. 10

Rockford:

I will not, at 4 in the morning, listen to public
utilities and assholes talking about civic responsibiity.
I don't give a damn about Wallace Beery; from what I hear
he ws not exactly a ladies' man – doesn't have to be.
I say there *were* no piranha in that government tank,
despite Viet Nam. The inevitable makes assholes of us all . . .
What *is* a 'saddle award'? Who *are* those people?

Oct. 18

Rockford:

My letters indicate that many of those who've
written me are dead: the radio works. Schumann stands
his own. Words hold, singularly appropriate. Balzac
doesn't move me much (pianos are yet that): Mendelssohn
either – it's the timbers. 60° is best temperature . . .
Signals vary.
    MAN, CENTER OF THE CONSTELLATION: our modus operandi.
With each case the same evidence.
Suffocating fish swim oily shores.
Green beans love sister-vegetation.
I applaud.
My regards to your lovely wife.

Oct. 7

Rockford:

Last night I read in bed, my right foot propped above
my head. This morning's mail is two weeks late: delivered
by a boy on a bicycle. The road is closed. The hill,
opposite, is a jagged sheet of flame. No wind – the fire
goes straight up, past a row of houses on stilts: like
yr letter, yet intact . . . Murder is wrong you say, 'killing
is necessary.'
    You were not born a cop. As a kid you played Tarzan.
Actors are on strike . . . Why aren't you picketing?

Oct. 21

Rockford:

I do not care for cars. You do. The thing to escape
(as you put it) flaunts itself daily. Obligations to
meet, glands taken in hand, bills paid. Beyond that,
it's Armageddon: people with shopping carts lined up
at the Safeway, five aisles deep, fighting for the last
of the sugar . . . The Mayor of Redlands has given orders
to shoot any fleeing Angeleno on sight.

Oct. 20

Rockford:

My neighbor across the road has given up BB's
for a Benjamin pump gun. Last night he shot at my
garbage cans. I agree with you about language. The
fires for the moment are out. Your father, you remind
me, is Wallace Beery's nephew, not his son. This fog
is everywhere: the sounds of words are an academic
matter. Our graphemes die with us.

Oct. 21

Rockford:

So I'm a coward: shoes wear out, boots are
needed in winter: my glasses, which I paid $20
for (wire rimmed), I have to keep on with bandaids.
It's not Merv Griffin who lives next door. Johnny
Carson didn't design this cabinet. My neighbor wants
a rifle. 'For protection,' he says.
You have seen the news?

No bombs went off . . . I was there. Orlene was sitting with
Max at the Hotel Ruhl. Nothing unusual: the traffic on
the Promenade brisk with bicycles, young people out for
a swim. New hats were paraded. A group of German poets
held seminar in the square.
I couldn't find the toilet.
A six-hour drudgery – a wan young lady in dark
glasses reading from ten volumes of her work, a gypsy-
like lady with too much mascara, a Turkish poet (who
writes in Turkish; is published in German and speaks
no English) and a clown of a man, perhaps thirty,
dressed in tails and top hat, who carried a rose.
I was at Little Joe's having a hamburger. Across
the road, the blind shop was closed; the guitar store
open. A garbage truck passed. Discussing his business
investments, Little Joe burnt my onions.
Cady found the reading dull: refused to sit.
Brigette sat. Sinclair was wearing her 'whore's shoes.'
We had a pitcher of beer, came back. When I did find
the toilet it was in use.
I used the urinal. Cady pissed in a booth.
Eva, Joe's wife, had emptied the coke crates and
was sweeping the sidewalk . . .

'Algerians,' Orlene said, and laughed: 'an invasion!'
Which turned out to be true: two airplanes few noticed,
dropping nine parachutists only newsmen saw, corner of
Fountain and Vista.

Nothing untoward on the face of it. The light changed.
A lady in curlers, crossing the street, pushes her shopping
cart into the laundromat. A bus stops.

'I practice,' says Eva, a plump cheerful woman: she
talks of her studies, 'I get better . . .

'Joe has his hamburgers. I have my music.'

Her ambition, she tells me, is to play with the
Fairfax Avenue Mandolin Orchestra.

Oct. 29

Ania:

Consider this a continuance: an hour's retainer
fee and $3 a day for the ladder I borrowed . . .

All morning my nextdoor neighbor is out chasing
mice with a pump gun: you tell *me* you spent $14 to
see The Sinking of The Titanic.

Nov. 4

Ania:

The worst is over? . . . It isn't here yet.
My car won't start. I just phoned the Auto Club.
Nobody answers.

This morning it was ground squirrels.

Homage
To A Lady

★

in cuban heels she walks high on
hallmark movies and demands to change
all channels for valium telling me
(god) she wants a catholic marriage
& hasn't been laid in 2 months what

★

silence pertains to the customary
performance she dresses up for 3 days
crying steadily because kent told her
to fuck off last night before the shrink
phoned today to tell her he couldn't

★

take her on as paying customer she
demands he be (without problems) a
nonsmoker over thirty-five
& happily married
not fat she says

Bagels

dizzy the two sides spill out
shouts for that aversion being
a thursday on the hands sweat
three pounds and ten plastic
bags brought home to dock

surreptitious as my slippery ass
paid ten bucks to haul out the garbage

★

warmed-over red satin sheets we
sweat yesterdays stopping oceans
at the side of the road humped
like fenceposts

making the act secure locks in the
bedroom thonged sandals under a pin-
ball machine beneath 5 acts the number
flashed neon & blue gas beneath or
atop yes the mouth upright

★

best health & a stout toast to
shine on each and every ramif-
ication words gobble up sense
to which the act stands perambu-
lating

★

get your foot off mine (under the table

And what does this sun do to us?
                    • • •
What President enjoyed pitching hay as a pastime?
Calvin Coolidge.
Playing Medicine-Ball? Herbert Hoover (aficionado).
Ju-Jitsu? Teddy Roosevelt.
        Benjamin Harrison I've also listed here:
plenty of fish still left in the stream for the
angler who has no rod. 'I never lost a little fish,
I never hope to lose one; neither fish nor flesh
nor good red herring.'

        What does it mean
the piping of the bats toward the horizon?

Six
For Paul

the footstep freezes in midair
discursive as photographs or cold cars
abandoning ship or loud talk
you bite your lip on

'a fieldmouse that sounds like
a rather large rat in the heater'

         • • •

       a shimmering mirage
       gods inside the hula-hoop
       rattling everyday goodbyes

       twelve songs across the road
       singing ukulele

         the metaphor.
      Intractable

mouth damp on the pillow.

A Death in the Family

Them eyes cut out –
Dotted perforations the lone Indian
Shot the end of war on linen tablecloths
        Sat upright to. Crawling on her hands & knees
        under the kitchen table with a butcher-knife.
One ett peas with a fork.

       •

        Popeye (without his pipe)
        And his lady –
            Maps for underwear.
            And two extra sets of legs
      for walking.

Observances
After D. M. Richardson

Walt will have a pacemaker put in at ten tomorrow morning.
    Ankles bear hard knocks. Ralph (Jesson) loses days
we drink to
and will buy lumber friday.
      Pianos are not catfood. Statements are lies.
            All statements are lies.

GALLANTRY
A Soap Opera in One Act

    Yes would be a lie. No would be a lie.
Any statement would be a lie. All state-
ments are lies. I like the Pernes better
than I like you. I like all of you better
than I like the Pernes. I hate you. I hate
the Pernes. I, of course you must know it,
hate *everybody*. I adore the Pernes so
much that I can't go and see them. But
you come and see us. Yes; but you insist.
Then you like us only as well as you like
the Pernes; you like all sorts of people
as well perhaps better than you like us.
I have nothing to do with anyone. You shall
not group me anywhere. I am everywhere.
Don't sit there worrying me to death.[1]

    .

all around the mulberry bush the monkey
chased

---

[1] in these rooms yes okay yes okay here
upright (again) das fick der flugel horn
don't make (necessarily) magic & jade
         flutes cowboys
leather stains you can't find
when you're busy looking

            halfway back to the ozarks i got
            no ear to
            godammit

NOTES FROM A WALLPAPERED BUS

'Frivolous in vice, unbelieving in passion Griselda sings about'
and Bismarck commended:

'Leave them only their eyes, that they might weep'

The cowboy poet nods, agrees.
then trots out mules (a withering thirst)
to stalk our ambiguities.

'Oh, him.

O, Fessel down the road –

Met me in the store, his packet of cigarettes tied in a
sleeveless lump of tee shirt,
and with a grin (at spying mirrors),
unzipped his pants in the aisle.'

Home Letters.
A Vaguely Ontological Aspiration
After Adriano Spatola

To write means to construct language, not to explain it.
— Max Bense

> Hope all are OK with you as we are
> here. Lee was over a few days let
> me know how things & everyone was
> at home Grace is OK had a bone out
> but Dr put it back. They never
> heard from Ron since he left the
> east. I had a letter from Grace she
> told me. Hon do you have $2.00 to
> spare I need a couple things. if
> not OK. Not much news here for now
> come home or write soon.

. . .

My work has been considered by some
to be 'politically disengaged' or
even 'para-hermetic.' Others, more
deliberately, have assumed a voc-
ation born of political motives
but tarnished by a confidence in
the power of poetry a little too
aristocratic and outmoded. Let us
try to look at these arguments closely.

A few lines hope every
thing is OK. And thanks
a million for the Xmas
gifts & your coming home
sure was nice only hate
to see you go when you
come. Had a phone
call from Eddie last nite
said he had been in Florida
in the Hosp with that
bleeding of the rectum
like he had before his
operation. He also wanted
$30. which we did not have
to telegraph him. Said he
would be home next Sunday.
He paid $1.85 to call me

I ask where he was wouldnt say I ask his address said he had none.
I tried to trace the call but they said they dont keep track of
the calls any more. So
I dont know whats all
this about. I told him
he better get home
& quit acting like
an ass. I ask him why
he went away said I
just dont know but
wanted to come home.

We say outright that we have no in-
tention of reviving, even if only
for the sake of controversy, the
old Italian dichotomy – political
engagement vs. disengagement. It is
rather symptomatic that this should
be brought up now in Italy, where the

He better with that
car out of state dont
know what mess he is
into now Healthwise.
better get home &
stop this.

one appearance of relief for poetry
(but not only for poetry) is a
balanced stagnation.

A note to let you know I havent heard anything from nobody
the Welfare is checking everything out seems funny no one
can find him or the car. I had a letter from Riverside
yesterday Eddie owes them money he collected on the trip
never turned it over
Collections from In-
surance & etc He sure
has made a mess this
time. Edward getting
himself in a mess
having a hell of a
time trying to get
married she is 15.
Her mother is no help
expects every one else
to solve the situation.
If I could get some
one to buy the living
room set for $125.00
& sell the rest to who
might need any thing I

On the other hand, if it is true
that my work has castled itself in
poetry, it is also true that this
happened not because it is the easiest
position to defend but because it is
through poetry that one may pose the
problem of language, a language capable
of concentrating on the symptoms of
reality.

have. The used furniture places said $300 for everything in
the house. I cant see T.V. & everything as the house stands
for that. can you. all this driving me bats.

We enter one of these crises with the intention of suggesting
new directions for poetry. Programmatic declarations are
always forced and naïve and often end up in confirming the
status quo. However, it is never useless to affirm the urgency
of a vertical restructuring of poetry, of a critical
distillation which is neither in complicity with, nor evasive
of the linguistic context provided by mass media.

. . . formulas worn-out from within.   I heard from Grace she
was to leave Hosp
yesterday May 13 Mothers
day. She is going to Bobs will be laid up two months more Xrays
to see how her hip healed before trying to walk. Her leg was
getting shorter had weights on but didnt work. So operated on

it some thing was wrong
they had to break it
over put a plate in.
She is allowed up 1
hr in her wheel chair has
to be lifted out of
bed. She wanted me to
come be with her I was
ready to go Helen wrote
she was moving to
3 rooms blue crying said

*Our decision to publish is oriented
toward the possibility of a poetry
which constructs itself as an objective
metamorphosis not a metaphorical
paraphrase of reality.*

Grace's hip was OK be around in 3 days. Grace was getting
childish. I know better than that she did not want me to come.
She didnt move. Her & Roy went to the cabin in Mts a wk last
wk. Make sure Grace went to Bobs as they would not release her
if no one was home. I'll
sure tell her a lot of
things. I'll go later if
Grace is able & wants to
I'll bring her here. Helen
Roan took inward hemorrages
yesterday they operated on
her right away. Dont know
full particulars. Ed's
working at Riverside gets
most every day in. Grace
got your card said she had
a good laugh about it. &
tell you thanks.

*Is my work, in its refusal of the
dichotomy, political engagement/
disengagement, a poetry based on
vaguely ontological aspirations?
And in its refusal of silence,
does it hide perhaps a pseudo
demiurgical need to render the
word sacred?*

Notes
In Passing

Some people didn't come.
    The church ws cold.
    I liked the tolling bell.
        we ate a Mexican lunch

Down the cliff
from the grave-site
a nude beach.

      smoked 3 packs of cigarettes
      (I put a carton on my plastic)

  •

Cunnilingus Institute does not exist.
Only Brooks. 2 stop signs, we got lost.

Cedar: varathaned.
He seemed a short man, not knowing him.
     12 hours, portal-to-portal.
I can't remember which
museum. The house is

  •

     gray gloves...
     Two priests stayed behind.
A lady poet couldn't get her car out.

An Educated Logic

demanded more than should be given.
the earthworm (resuscitated) put
on a turntable to get its color back.

read George Sand (Farley Granger's cousin),
saw Red Shoes six times
and recently found out Hedy Lamarr
once lived in this apartment

• • •

monotonies of plot and catholic ghosts
a discussion of (maeterlinck & napoleon)
extracted arguments of style
plutarch had something to do with
Histories
            left muddled as to origin
            and stanza.

            the war of 1812 (played tchaikovsky)
            guns dismantled the sisters bronte
            (did something) & brothers and sisters
            Italian wrote (sonnets) starched dresses
            crinoline smoked cigars (unlikely for
            ladies) amy lowell stalked glass thru
            her garden (at beverly hills high) where
            once Edith Sitwell read

                        her brooch hit the microphone

Letter

The christian name makes impossible
any face-front exchange of plain talk.
The remedy (as I've sd before) runs
amok the chittering squirrels on roof-
tops & owls (tail-balanced) hung from
trees. Adjectives kill, or stultify
and, in any case, belabor the room
we so carefully establish. Privacy
hs everything to do with it – topical –
and them day-old sausages brought (un-
wanted) to the door we eat anyway,
threshold and lintel.

You tell me we have five years to
change the language. I wonder what
you mean. Me? Us? Why? and what's
to change? Maybe you didn't say
'change the language' but we hd 5
years. My overalls will be washed
fifteen times by then, some shredded
for lawn chairs; the rest abused &
at least one pair given my dentist
as collateral . . . Poetic endowments
(? To be sure) get me in fistfights
at parking lots.

Swamp
Two Pieces on Wittgenstein

I

The swamp had to be cleared of brittle weeds
and rusted teakettles.
          'Bombed out, wind-sucked to ground zero.'
The head gone, the rest buried.
(Somewhere the picture of him with a lump hardon –
how she got flushed when he did that – like that
once at the restaurant – fiddled up her dress
with his tennis shoe)
          Them days ws done.
          'You didn't snatch that young cock –
and or orifice, red-lipped warm and willing.
          He was not willing.
          But hell, you didn't seem to want it anyway.
          Being he ws eighteen, in bed to begin with.
Waiting for it . . .

          'Babbling, you are babbling.'
The Colonel stood watching. Twenty of those
'ruffian' (how he sd the word) soldiers gangfucked
before their memory went. 'Shanty songs –'
          Midway between a tar dock and an uptown
bank of cattails.

*

Dead now of course, his best friends sd so:
wanted three things – to get married,
make a baby and commit suicide.
Wrote haiku, fucked and exploded.

          'Logic, man.' The Colonel ws adamant.
'Can't tell a man by his eyes.'
I am my car, I am my christmas pajamas.

Tackiest part of the enterprise put hives on yr ass.

2

Pills?
A razor blade?
'Here man,' sd the Colonel, 'stop whining.'
          Needed to hold he sd, and wasn't inclined.
          Had to have a woman.
          'Can't tell a man by his eyes.'

Cornholing ws nothing you did in knickers.
drolly standing in.
    'I am my car.
I am my christmas pajamas.'

got him on the bed, serenaded mendelssohn records
plowed it in (his head caught under the doorsill)
and burnt his elbows on the carpet.
    'Shanty songs –'
midway between a tar dock & an uptown bank of cattails.
Doubtless well endowed . . .
    Dead now of course, best friends agreed.
    Wanted three things: to get married
    make a baby and commit suicide.
Wrote haiku, fucked and exploded.

    '$A = A_2$.'
    A cow is not.
    Tackiest part of the enterprise put hives on yr ass:
the creaking shoes, the itchy shirt that never fit him.
Stones were stones. The Colonel ws adamant:
    'Do it asshole.'
    Then send boxes of caramels.

Swan Song
To Ithaca

'The fact of it is,' she sys
as to when 'things are finished'
those long syntactical strides
fence posts hide in

      a 49 ford the roof blew off
      this side palm springs

      •

      first class from chicago cd she come

      •

'importunately averse to'
(lovers flung down steps
      with broken flower pots)

      Days off with roses,
      three nights running.

      • • •

her daughter is at yale she sys.
'where we should have gone.'

      •

      the boy, now grown,
      lives in beverly hills somewhere,
      and must certainly look italian.

Homage to Paul Vangelisti
upon the publication of
"Reading the Masters"

Paul Vangelisti

Reading the Masters
MVCCLH
Gof in Singapore

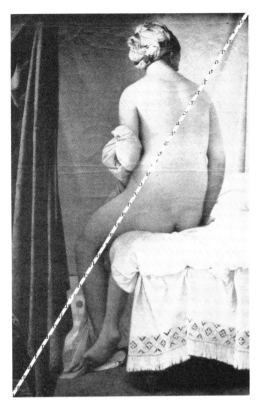

Ingres: *Bather* (1808)

Courbet: *Proudhon and His Daughters* (1865)

Degas: *Studies of Manet* (1865)

Manet: *Bar at the Folies Bergères* (1881)

Renoir: *Dance at Bougeval* (1883)

Seurat: *La Grande Jatte* (1884-86)

Cézanne: *The White Sugar Bowl* (1890-94)

Matisse: *Madame Matisse* (1905)

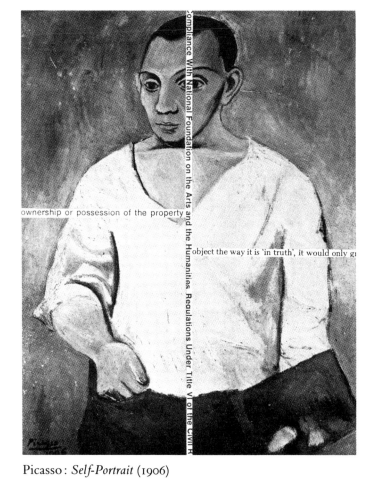

Picasso : *Self-Portrait* (1906)

Photo of Duchamp (1965)

[*"Reading the Masters" was
cut & composed in 1979*]

M V C C L H

'The observer is the past.'
— Crazy Horse

by now nobody but nobody
if not asleep or unpacking equipment
follow the dust and mountain tops
hoping to settle someplace quick
where it doesn't rain much
and next to all the water in the world

★

ought to have been here yesterday
morning was up sudden and windless
not much talk everybody to work
just doing where they should
humming and whistling
by noon it's all rolling and
more than half the village burned down

★

go on pilgrim
how precarious does it feel
out here beneath the page
can't be much worse than spring
one minute looking at desert
next can't find shadow for the water
and that vertigo the
sheer drop between what you see
and what you say you see
anyhow means nothing but lots of big rock
mesquite and moving weather
hell almost been a week since we last saw our shadows

★

says after the War especially
the river hardly flows the valley
downstream is mostly mud and trickle
says chasing tequila shots with beer
how much the operation reminds of one Buddy Doar
biggest and slowest according to him

farmhand in eastern Kentucky
entering the barn one evening
interrupts Buddy bareass behind a cow
overalls at the ankles
drilling her like a Ford V-8
when Buddy notices he stops
not lifting his pants but picks up a shovel
waddles to the front and smashes her right between the horns
then without a word he arranges himself
ambling to the house to wash

*

a chopper lifts in the writer
reminding everybody he shakes hands with
'just to have one last look'
struts like he owns us
with that fat nosey voice
nobody gives a damn just that it talks at you
like the voice isn't his
'Commitment, Meaning, Destiny
out here in all this Wilderness'
as he finishes off the boss with a wink
and 'keep an eye on things'
backing and waving into the whirl of sand

*

hard to recall where it's moving
11 years ago a certain cruel innocence
a beauty in that fire burst dazzling
red rose petals on the village below
or that thing as he named it
tiny fist of a thing eating from inside
11 years ago hard to say about the boundaries
so much moving so much lost now
hardly nothing out here seems to end

*

repeats sleep good last night pilgrim
adjusting himself around a glass
can't get the operation off his mind
animals jammed in the trailers kicking and biting
all that ammunition and fire wasted

on some village nobody's going to need
worked around it maybe even rested the day
still the night attack to do upriver
time he finally gets to sleep
dreams of an old woman like his grandmother he says
but darker moving her lips in some prayer or explanation
with left hand cupped above her right
as if holding something then stops
to give a big smile and reverses her hands
turning that invisible upside down

*

no move now almost five days of meetings
briefings more meetings
scrub trucks and personnel carriers
wash underwear sweep out and rearrange the tents
somehow all sort of permanent
lots of talk and drunk memories of back home
being forgotten out here
a few break down curse the operation
wives girlfriends women in general
till they strip naked running through camp
and jump in the river
sobbing and hopeless drunk
in that two feet of muddy water
maybe some movement tomorrow
another place new page

*

still here though weather's just about splendid
low 70s wind and clouds from the northeast
mountains afloat swapping shape and color
mesquite sage even cactus burst flowers
most take sun hardly drinking
nobody would believe how many shades of gray and blue

*

what you believe pilgrim could fit a thimble
who wants it out here
only nobody's got anything better
opened a letter from back home
and at the end says about the neighbor kid

can't be more than 17
one morning about a month ago now
kid dresses all in black
with one of those Halloween skull masks
and out on the boulevard during rush hour
he hangs himself from a stoplight
nobody trying to get the kid down
just gawking and speeding on to work

★

strange the last few weeks
don't notice but the words you become
so embarrassing to see them being kind
the loud desperate talk the old days
to a man they knew
until it's too late all comes to a dead stop
just the crickets and the river
and maybe a 'later' or 'thanks'
tossed over the shoulder as you stand in the dark
half drunk and sleepy not wanting to go to bed
to wake tomorrow everywhere in the same place

★

nobody talking much
try to sleep or write letters
weather's good but the liquor almost gone
no whiskey or tequila just three beers each a day
hardly see the boss in his tent all the time meeting
ought to be a half moon in a few hours
take a little smoke and beer ration upstream
maybe forget to think about it
leaning on a few thousand stars

★

more rumor of the move upriver and the night attack
nobody sleeps late all singing and joking
like the first week out here
some even mention the end of the operation
and back home and the first thing they're going to do
until around noon when it started to rain
been almost five days of hard rain cold damp nights

back in the tents so quiet makes you want to scream
to think of another letter another page
and nothing else in this goddamn windy dark

★

happens like nobody dreamed it
the morning up sudden and windless
not much talk everybody to work
noon the first trucks roll into the new camp upriver
by four setting it all up for the night attack
and the old man orders to break out what's left of the beer

★

lanterns on the hood of the truck
a corporal named Walker stands on the bumper
whipping them up so desperate they're almost in tears
'*Why do you obey like slaves and kiss your lieutenant's ass? Yes, sir, yes, sir,
when half of you are almost old men, full of scars and mutilated, serving 20 or
30 years out here in this waste. Hard winters and hard working summers, ugly
war and even uglier peace. What do you have to look forward to? Retirement?
A letter from some senator congratulating you? A few years left of sitting on
the porch waiting for your government check, in a town full of people whisper-
ing, "Ain't been the same since he's been back. Not the nice sociable fella we
used to know." And right now we're out here in the middle of nothing, fighting
an enemy we can almost smell but never see, dying one by one in our sleep or
at the latrines if you're stupid enough to have to sneak a crap in the middle of
the night . . . '*

★

he comes forward
hardly waiting for the corporal to finish
'*It's hard to stand here among you. I feel a deep sadness because I have no idea
what to even call you. Friends is not the looks on your faces as I walked up
here. Soldiers is not the hysterical shouting of savages I hear in my own camp
when real savages wait out there for you all to get tired of your little fun and
fall asleep. Maybe you're the kind who like to stand in a crowd and cheer some
nobody who's telling you exactly what he thinks you want to hear. In this
Army we call that kind a* civilian! *So, if I'm offending any of you soldiers, I
truly apologize. I came here to say that I'll be available in my tent till mid-
night to discuss any aspect of this operation.*'

★

slice of burnt orange moon in June
and all the rest of that horseshit
long time hadn't heard it spoken like last night
so bright and shining when he said *soldiers*
standing tall in the lantern light
in front of those trucks like a Caesar
hushing them all with a single word

★

a little way upriver from camp
six years ago the slaughter of three whole divisions
all hats off in that damp arroyo
not even the old man finding words
on the open ground bleached bones
scattered at the first retreat
piled high as houses where they made a stand
on the scraggly pine like ornaments
skulls grinning five or six to a branch
and the worst those trenches or pits
oldtimers call them 'altars'
where senior officers were tortured and butchered
here the limbs and skulls mashed so nobody could look long
soon we all have shovel in hand
covering over six years of rotting shame
even the old man pitches in
eyes full of tears like the rest
not knowing what he's burying belongs to a stranger or a friend

★

sleep good last night pilgrim
adjusting himself around a glass
dreamed again of that old woman
like his grandmother he says but darker
this time she's in the middle of all this he doesn't want to see
kept shutting his eyes but the old woman's always there
holding out her hand like she's in some painting or movie
coming right out of the frame
and he can't wake up
every time he opens his eyes she's there reaching
and he finally takes the old woman's hand as he says
so goddamn cold and small he wants to cry
and pushes her away till he's awake

★

barely a week or so to moving out
after the night attack nobody's been sober much
slapping each other on the back
all the time grinning
something almost fierce in the joy of those whistles and songs
afternoons longer now not a lot to do
artillery already on the way out
plenty of tequila and smoke till the end of the operation
seems earlier every day to wander upstream
and climb the spine of the arroyo
smelling the sage looking down
on soft running shoulders of mesquite and chaparral
hell don't even wait for dusk to start counting stars

★

it's like inventing them
a star for everything you never did
each time looking into the blaze of sunset
you wipe that sky clean
don't even get tired of it
except for an occasional want of writing her
three years worth of letter
loose and careless as this afternoon
read once how a writer said he got peaceful
watching the big animals at the zoo
elephants or hippopotamus
for me hills and mountains in the growing dusk
and all the things I'll never be

★

thinking of the explorers and settlers who passed through
not very long ago maybe two or three hundred years
hardly any time at all in this country
according to the old timers
you can lose a village out here in 30 years
always wondered the direction the destiny of those people
to keep them holding on through such terrible wind and sun
sometimes have to think twice to even remember your mother's name
just the opposite of back home
where everything's because of what people did
out here there's nobody watching
just you and all that sky inside

★

turned real hot yesterday
morning was up heavy and windless
nobody even trying the little work left
by 10 most of us upstream dabbling our toes
searching for shade under the spine of the arroyo
by 11 that shade's moving faster than the sun
like some huge hand the palm yawning and relentless
and down there in the tent
the old man in khaki shirt and pants
sweating his final dreams

*

sunset awesome in this heat
receding ablaze like an eye squeezes shut
pulling you with it there at the core
the sleepless heart of that watching dark and immemorial
like a boy first on fire with the idea of China
stares out at the Pacific
all the way on the other side

*

nobody sleeping much
waiting around like birds to take flight
hardly any difference night from day
just the dark and slow cooling
even now sense it gather behind that towering range
as if you're tied to it
and nothing to do but follow and follow
inside and scorching out

*

all this talk of sleepless dreams
must be the heat
by now nobody but nobody
too many miles and years away
always noon and the mountain tops
hoping to leave for someplace quick
and next to all the water in the world

*

Gof in Singapore

and a voice is more often a voice of outside the voice is as she screams turning left in front of a hot May Friday 4:30 in the 'Wait for me' as she screams hunger without appetite silence with no margin for the thirsty faces the crowding as she screams Wafer me away from the page that was sacrificed this afternoon

★

he misses the bus more often than not he remembers what he forgot to say and is left with having to forget the living to remember to scream stop the bus and let my brother Jack more often than not the page is ripped out as the hands are read and remembered in the dark rocking trolley as all the lights go off and outside the voice it's bright midnight tentative little indians ago who never screams get a job

★

did he miss the bus or not says she
felicitous as a snake in rayon
the phone rings he loses his place
she dials a number no one answers
the bus is packed he has to fart
she changes the subject he doesn't dare
the phone rings a page is missing
can't reach the cord it blows away
misses his stop she changes the subject
doesn't dare the bus is packed
the phone rings a page is missing

★

it blew away but not that simple
a necktie maybe or an old friendship
depending on the choice of sunsets
what's left to hold the sox up
a nostalgia or even a rage for justice
as the metaphors now seem nothing more
loud bands lots of heroes cheap gas
a piece of cake as they demonstrate in Singapore

★

is it to keep alive
that luminous torso that radiant step
when the slope above the freeway is alive
pubic with mesquite and chaparral
do we remember the words
do we keep our dead understood
and dancing parenthetically
as sparrows dance those ripe tunes
in foggy hibiscus

★

is it strictly for the record for the living who make a living playing the
record backwards who incriminate the whispers they couldn't fear in
case the singer is without a song as she cuts in front of this mute Friday
voiceless behind her windshield mouthing words she never thought to
mouth Wafer me as she plays her car backwards into the parking lot
rolls up her window screaming what she couldn't hear

★

literally it was a week ago

what she couldn't hear was the quiet of this table

what she didn't know would destroy her

how she was dressed doesn't matter

that it was Friday afternoon and her about 30 was
    convenient

that it's a glass table is worth mentioning

that it gleams with accusation is redundant

why the bare leg and slipper under the table look
    so disembodied isn't really important

that she blocked traffic to push a button to slide
    her window down to scream what she screamed is
    only coincidental

it was literally one week ago he had to fart and a
    page was missing

★

windows still dirty birdsong acute
everything else shrinks in the ripening wind
lavender pickup garbage cans mailman
telephone ringing in the next room
and the luminous torso the radiant step
naming the motion of the oak
as it removes all movement but memory

★

as if one poises to plunge that perfect whiteness
when the page is in fact not white
and anybody's business but the living
because the birds won't shut up the knee hurts so
he's furious at even the thought of yesterday or her
changing the subject as he considers chasing the bus

★

the ache revises the birdsong more acute
the writing fast and sloppier
dove swoop the size of a pigeon
the street outside is nobody's business
indian brush and oak and tile roofs
stir terribly slow as a Sunday afternoon
when all vision subsides to ash
and mother rises to answer the telephone

★

he moves to the kitchen easy as breath
she hands him parenthetically a cup of coffee
they talk of gophers or cacti or Wittgenstein
she asks if he wants to hear her dream
anybody in the rest of the house is sound asleep
they talk of gilia or desert or Husserl
he says he'd like to go fishing soon
she carefully describes letters she avoids writing
the phone rings a page is ripped out
it's years before they talk of dreams again

★

Connemara Delphi Kinshasa Corlaga Fundy Manhattan
Fort-Lamy or Perth

they often appear to be looking straight ahead the cord
missing

or every few weeks the small anonymous envelope of rubber
bands from Van Nuys

not mornings of eager light brief passages and gliding
etc.

or cancelled checks from Singapore always made out to
cash always those inkstains under the signature

★

they circle not seeming to move the feet
only eyes and lips splendid with hunger
the phone rings as the throat is cut
the page ripped out as blood covers the hands
and the voices approach call out names
he tries to remember the words
the radiant step the phone rings
as they circle thirst like flame
does he dare to sing

★

Bath Bangkok Bamabo Baikal. The phone stops. His hands are red.
Even birthday greetings from Patagonia, six months late, unsigned: a
worn looking penguin squints on the front of the card, some script
inside praising 'Gof and Gof's children.' The phone rings again. The
eyes are wide open. And of course the cancelled checks, regular as the
familiar almost paw-like stain under the signature. The phone stops.
The room and furniture seem larger. Sobat Satahip Sugari Singapore
Solo Shan.

★

the room photographs somewhat empty the furniture a
little worn and oversize

everything quite neat though as if arranged once more
at the last minute

some faces look almost smug fingers around half-empty
glasses but no legs crossed

their hands all the same none match the heads and seem
larger than they should

that the table gleams slightly isn't remarkable

the phone they said rang twice then stopped

one definitely needs a shave quite a few have their
shoes off

it's been more than a week now the time of day probably
makes no difference

most of all the eyes seem relieved tranquil marmorial or
just startled by the propriety of the instant

*

a household of names and dates unfurnished except for a few platitudes
and a funeral someone keeps mentioning nobody's in the kitchen shav-
ing and only his daughter runs through the garden anyhow time accu-
mulates rumor persists even if most endings remain minor and the
reader to blame again for being reread

*

It was crowded and too dark. The clock above the door read six sharp
but it had to be a lot later. The hatcheck girl made funny little smiles at
my tall package and me but I ignored her. Most of them were there, at
tables in the corners, trying not to be conspicuous. They looked the
other way and the smart people they sat with kept on chattering.
Sometimes you get a hunch what the talk is about but this place was
different. I worked the package and myself casually as I could toward a
couple of empty seats and Whitman at the end of the bar. Nice thing
about Walt, he was always where you expected. For instance, trying to
maneuver some amateur into a devastating contradiction or at least a
compliment or two and a free beer. Anyhow, muscular freshmen from
Princeton weren't what I'd come for so I slapped old Walt on the back,
got him to laugh that laugh of his and took a stool on his other side.
Mostly got a lot of Walt's shoulder which was just fine with me. As I
said the next stool was empty but on the bar in front of it almost a full
glass sat like some kind of shrine. Strawberries, champagne, etc. In
Paris they call it a Nymphe, in Rome a Paradiso. Don't know why but

I got so curious I almost reached over and touched it. When its owner walked up I flinched as if I had. It wasn't so much the surprise but the fact she took my breath away. Five-ten in loafers, long blond hair, no makeup, straight nose, high forehead, and those gray eyes. They had more than a touch of smoulder to keep you mesmerized and exquisite enough for no one else to notice. Pure class. Didn't even inquire about the package, just if I might not want to prop it in the corner next to her, which I did. Her talk was effortless or maybe it was the way she got me going. She asked questions and more than once I was amazed at my answers. She must have ordered another one of those drinks because I found the thing in my hand toasting who knows what. No matter how hard I try, it's only been a week, I can't remember at all what we said. It was more like a dance than anything else. She led and I followed and I didn't give a damn. Anyhow, at that point, right after the toasts, something happened. I glanced over toward Whitman and was a little surprised. Instead of grinning and well on his way, Walt was quiet, elbows on the bar, kind of examining his beer. The kid looked at Walt as if he'd said something and was expecting an answer. Somehow that made me nervous. I started to look around at the tables. They were gone. Strangers had taken their places, sat at their chairs. I needed to talk and they disappeared. As I turned back to her, I swear I felt something coming. She looked at me with a question on that perfect face of hers. If she spoke I didn't hear. I was in no mood for conversation. The bar rail under my feet was pitching and rolling and I knew I'd never learn the steps. I started to reach for my package. She was smiling and had her arms around me, breaking my fall, when the lights went out.

★

a small breeze again this morning
though the sparrows are already quiet
traffic hums a sign along the dry hills
it's mid-July postcard flesh on roller skates
the Pacific about 17 miles to the southwest
he stares from the doorway
tomorrow he dreams of never having known you before

GEOGRAPHIES

let the ships be quiet.
don't linger here : them
3 part-time soldiers
(lopsided) saluting last taps
recorded atop a carnival van

don't linger that plastic grass
can be used again, limp across
another hole of a gravestone
we celebrate good will

and rooms stay rooms
we need to live in

don't linger
here

★

At five he said he wd grow up to remember it, that feeling he had
that he wasn't expected to be there children are not expected to be
there they just happen and he was not really a child, he knew that &
he resolved that one day he wd tell them that little pitchers have big
ears that they are expected to be seen & not heard was horseshit it
was all horseshit and still is worrying about the telephone bill (for
example) and the latest bank statement
        which is what makes romance
        when there is none and few scientists around to
keep up the description stein said that not me
and she's right people don't understand that

voices don't need spoken to talk any kid
knows that i did that's what makes secrets
& words so hard to catch it takes years
sometimes

i am still learning all that
i knew in the first place

★

Robert Crosson

A first book consisting of 'William James', 'Gertrude Stein', 'General
Booth' & 'Ives'. 1980, 80pp, $4.

Epopœia and
the Decay of Satire

The poem is a true & rooted cactus

after all the
mirages incident to
desert, these apparent
                    lakes with such
                    apparent water birds &
                    whispering reeds
                    after all these
                    images
                              that seduce in the
                              far air
                              & dry the tongue to black &
                              kill
after these / but in the
geographic foreground
this true & rooted cactus
most real & tough
with thorns
rooted in the genuine dry
                         having sucked deep
                         & with its toughness held
                         held
its thorns make blood
hands & lips
but cut into that
leather fruit
& the water is truly there
tasting green

John Thomas

How does one review the work of a poet who mocks the societal role of the poet, who has no desire to publish his poetry and says that he has no interest in the familiar moral values of poetry and poets? Especially when that poet happens to be writing some of the best poetry of our times and reads his poems publicly more convincingly than Dylan Thomas did, with less sonority and theatricality. And, moreover, a poet whose views about politics, love, male and female relationships and psychedelics are sometimes shockingly noncontemporary and often contradictory. In a word, unfashionable. Perhaps the best way to begin is to let him speak in his own voice, the unmistakably personal voice of the mature poet, sure of himself, and not caring a damn if you find the voice unfamiliar and quite different from anyone or anything you have taken for granted as poetry, modern or traditional.
                                                    – Lawrence Lipton

(1976, 56pp, $3.50)

Paul Vangelisti

. . . .

cockroach under my typewriter
hesitate my fingers
listen to the words
to the voice of the word 'cockroach'
like a face for women in another car
tip of my finger stare at what surrounds you
the reader barely possible

air

. . . .

0 PORTFOLIO

Event 21 : . . . and forces Xerox copies of the poetry of Dylan Thomas on his friends. In flight Los Angeles to San Francisco the very young and the very old continue looking down. The rest scanning vinyl-bound magazines and reports, the 'suchness' of progress the pure habits of investment the sound of flight in the sound of pages turned lips puckering to sip the vodka the icy cigarette. Perhaps if he had not been asked to narrate and compose music for a television documentary about adopted children in search of their natural parents . . .

ANOTHER YOU

"a willing suspension of apples
bobbing like friars in the grass
what's the score
why always steel blue eyes to love
does it hurt anymore to slice
little women from the disbelief
of yet another pose of roses"

Air: 1973, 52pp, $2.50.
Portfolio (with *The Tender Continent*): 1978, 56pp, $4 paper, $10 cloth.
Another You (including *The End of the Game*, a verbal-visual collaboration with Adriano Spatola & Giulia Niccolai): 1980, 64pp, $4 – a Nov. 1981 selection of the Small Press Book Club: *"This collection of pieces, poems, collaborations is a fair overview of the unsettling and distinguished work of Paul Vangelisti . . . all characterized by the same surprise of image, the same unsettling shifts that mark his work"*

Invisible City

HUMPS & WINGS

A selection of Polish poetry since '68.
Edited by Tadeusz Nyczek, translated by
Boguslaw Rostworowski & illustrated by
Jan Sawka. Including Krzysztof Karasek,
Stanislaw Baranczak, Adam Zagajewski,
Julian Kornhauser, Ryszard Krynicki &
Antoni Pawlak. (80 pp, paper $5)

*'68 marked the beginning in poetry of the drama
of silent shouting. The dream of loud silence.
The reasoning of the poets was challenged by
reasons of censorship and reasons of state . . .
Tongues got stiffer and a false language was
broadcast by anonymous mouths that, in 'the name
of the nation' flooded the daily papers.* 'From
our voice they will compose other voices' . . .

Italian Poetry, 1960–1980: from Neo to Post Avant-garde

To Open

*Nothing behind the door, behind the curtain,
the fingerprint stuck on the wall, under it,
the car, the window, it stops, behind the curtain,
a wind that shakes it, a more obscure. . . . . . .*

— Antonio Porta

edited by Adriano Spatola & Paul Vangelisti; some 77 visual & linear poets
from Accame to Xerra. 128pp; cloth $12.50, paper $7.50.
From the editors' intro: *"In this collection certain texts are difficult
readings while others prove difficult to interpret, even though they might
appear at first more accessible. In Italian poetry of the last 20 years,
direct language is not always spoken language, and indirect language is
not always that of the written word."*

the first 25

A condensation of the first 25 issues of the tabloid *Invisible City*; since 1971, an eclectic collection of poems, translations, visuals & statements, published whenever enough good material is available (the zero volume, late '83). *"There's alot of visibility here, and the streets are well-paved and full of unexpected delights."*
                                                                    – Robert Peters

Direct orders to: Red Hill Press
                  PO Box 2853
                  San Francisco CA 94126
All our titles are available from Small Press Distribution
1784 Shattuck Ave, Berkeley CA 94709
Some of the book-series *Invisible City* are available from
BOOKPEOPLE (2940 Seventh St, Berkeley CA 94710)
Our tradelist of over 50 titles is available upon request.
SSAE appreciated.